FINAL SCORE: BOYS 8 GIRLS 3

FAMILY STORIES AS RECALLED BY DAVE AND CAROL KERZIE WITH CONTRIBUTIONS FROM THEIR CHILDREN

by
DAVE AND CAROL KERZIE

authorHOUSE™

1663 LIBERTY DRIVE, SUITE 200
BLOOMINGTON, INDIANA 47403
(800) 839-8640
WWW.AUTHORHOUSE.COM

First published by AuthorHouse 11/16/05

ISBN: 1-4208-7726-7 (sc)

Library of Congress Control Number: 2005907381

Printed in the United States of America
Bloomington, Indiana

This book is printed on acid-free paper.

Numerous illustrations including the cover sketch by Matthew Kerzie; others by Dave Kerzie.

TABLE OF CONTENTS

INTRODUCTION

Final Score: Boys 8 – Girls 3 is a book about a family. This family is unique in that it is a somewhat larger in numbers than most. In the nineteenth, and first part of the twentieth century, large families were not unusual in America. After all, somebody had to take care of the crops and the harvest. By the time we came along, the concept of the normal family consisted of a mom and dad and two kids. Our courtship commenced in the middle 50s, when the norm seemed to be a family of four. We talked about having a large family, however, and we found it relatively easy to conceive. We love children and listened to others on how to raise kids as well as developing ideas of our own. Carol was especially strong and dedicated her life as a mother. Elvis helped start a social revolution about the time we were married and we grew up with our eleven children from the late 50s all through the wondrous changes of the 60s, 70s, 80s, and first part of the 90s.

The story of this family takes place over an extended period of forty or more years. There is no real ending, as there are enough offspring to create following generations for centuries. The forty years can be separated into halves. The first is from Dad and Mom's courtship through a period of about twenty years. It was during this period that all eleven children were born and the family led the life as gypsies. Moving was the way of the military family and stakes were pulled no less than fourteen times. The second period occurs after

Dave's retirement from the service and coincides with his employment in industry. This chapter, again a time period of approximately two decades, is relatively stable as the domicile consisted of one home for this entire time. The pros and cons from our viewpoint, with respect to an unsettled environment versus a stable one, are addressed later. A third chapter could be written for the period in which we are living at the present time. This takes place after the last "little one" leaves home and Dad and Mom have finally retired from their jobs. Is there a fourth chapter or period? We are sure there is. Only time will tell.

The book consists of a series of short stories and anecdotes. Dave (Dad) writes most, as he remembers the various occurrences and adventures. Other inputs come from Carol (Mom), and still others from the children as they recall from memory their youth. An enormous mistake was that a diary was not maintained and therefore a great deal of excellent material was lost through the years. But then, who had time to write a daily diary?

Some of the stories are meant to be amusing and others are more serious, and all are written with a certain amount of nostalgia. We hope that when you read some of the material that you recognize some of the things we found useful in raising a family. The bottom line is that there is no substitute for love of each other and faith in God.

HOW IT ALL STARTED

DAVE'S NOTE

She was sixteen the first time I saw her. At least, I think that was the first time, for we grew up most of our early years living less than two miles apart. The reason we probably didn't meet earlier is that we attended different schools. Carol went to parochial schools and I to public schools.

Every story has a beginning. Our story began through a "close encounter" at a bus stop. The story of this encounter and early romance was documented in the *Antelope Valley Press* in 1994. It is reproduced with a couple of updates below.

THE SCHOOLGIRL AT THE BUS STOP

I am really a romantic at heart. The story I have to tell is about the initial encounter of my spouse and myself and our ensuing courtship. The story may not ring "romance" to all readers but it means a great deal to me. The significance of our love affair is written in the last paragraphs, which I think you will find very profound.

The year was 1954. I had just entered the university and was commuting every day from my parents' home to

1

campus in a 1939 Ford. During one particularly fine fall day, the car was in the shop and my only remaining source of transportation was the mass transit bus system. After school, while approaching the off-campus bus stop for my trip home, I took particular note of a young schoolgirl waiting for her ride. So long ago - yet, I remember vividly her long shoulder-length hair, yellow sweater, and plaid skirt. Her face was beautiful - not unlike Ann Blyth or Ava Gardner, two of my favorites at the time. There was something about her poise and manner that really hit me hard. As fate would have it - we both boarded the same bus and transferred to the same second bus. She did not notice me even though a close seating arrangement was achieved through a considerable amount of judicious footwork on my part.

In those days, we were taught that one did not initiate a conversation with a person of the opposite sex unless properly introduced. She obviously did not notice the enamored young man's many glances, for eye contact was never established.

All was not lost, however, as note was taken where the young maiden left the bus and also the design of the covered textbooks she carried in her arms.

The book covers were of a university located in another part of our city. I knew that she looked a little young for a college coed and thought maybe she attended an academy prep school for the college matching the emblem of her book jackets. My cousin had attended that same academy. Sure enough - after a few minutes of looking through her school annual -the mystery girl's picture was found. Her name was Carol. A beautiful name to match a pretty lady! A little research in the local directory provided her exact address and telephone number.

Still, a proper introduction had to be arranged. My cousin did not know the girl and so, I was still left to my own imagination and resources. As weeks and months passed, and while dating several other girls, my mind often flashed back to the girl at the bus stop. Eventually, frustration took the place of logic and common sense. Knowing her bus schedule, I would occasionally drive by the stop or her home hoping to just catch a glimpse of her. I suppose it became obvious after a while because she started to take notice.

It was almost a year later - another beautiful fall afternoon - when fate played its hand once again. After shooting a few baskets at a local school playground, the pretty face crossed my mind, as it had done many times before.

A drive-by cruise on the street by her home was initiated. En route however, I found most readily that two automobiles traveling a course line perpendicular to each other couldn't occupy a city street intersection at the same moment. A short time later, as the tow truck hauled my precious car away, and while sitting in the back of the black and white, I caught her glance of concern from the small crowd of onlookers.

3

Was I going to let all this hard work, planning, and circumstance go for naught? Not this guy! The next day's class schedule was adjusted to permit my arrival at the university bus stop at you-know-what time. I was so nervous as her eye caught mine that I felt weak all over. "Mr. Cool" prevailed however with an, "Oh, were you there?" response when she asked about the car. We made light conversation all the way to where Carol left our bus. I phoned her a week later and she accepted my invitation for our first date. We treat October 8, 1955 almost like an anniversary.

A wonderful courtship lasted three years and we were married one month after my university graduation. Carol is my bride, wife, and lover. She is also my best friend and pal. Most noteworthy of our marriage, besides our love, is our eleven children. All the kids have graduated from college and we are convinced that all our children are (or will be) positive contributors to society.

I often think back to that first day when I fell in love with Carol as she was standing there on the bus stop. Everything seems to have a purpose. I say a prayer of thanks to the good Lord every day, for it must have been He who drove us together that beautiful fall afternoon. Yes, I do believe in the magic of love at first sight.

HOW IT MIGHT HAVE ENDED
BEFORE IT REALLY STARTED

We were married 17 January, 1959. Dave had orders to report for active duty to the United States Air Force and nine days later, with all our worldly possessions packed in the trunk and back seat of our little car, together with a few hundred dollars, we departed for San Antonio, Texas.

Dave's first assignment was for a month-long orientation. A motel was located not too far from the entrance gate of the base and arrangements were made for an extended stay. A retired army nurse, who seemed like a very nice lady, managed the motel. She was married to a retired GI who also seemed nice, but he looked and acted a little rough around the edges. We were very young at that time, newlyweds on a honeymoon yet, and probably very naive.

We were becoming settled, when in the middle of our third night, probably about 2AM or so, a very loud knock was heard on the motel door. Dave got up, cracked the door, and found the motel man rambling and raving that the police were after him. He wanted Dave to come outside and take care of his problem. The "gentleman" was obviously stoned out of his mind. Dave complied to keep the peace. The police didn't show up, and the guy finally went back to his motel unit. Needless to say, sleep didn't come too easily for the remainder of that night.

To say the least, the young couple was kind of wary for the remainder of the stay, although the motel manager and her husband seemed reasonably sociable.

That was until the night before the departure for our next assignment. About bedtime, again, another knock was heard at the door. This time it was the motel lady asking for help. Dave went with her to their unit and found her husband in bed, delirious, ranting and raving, and completely out of control. He finally settled down as the medical aid arrived. The medics gave him a shot (or whatever they do for those that are inebriated and in need of help), and the nightmare was left behind us as we motored off early the next morning.

That was not the end of the story, however. Several months later, we had gone out for Sunday morning breakfast in Laredo, Texas, where we were stationed at the time. A San Antonio newspaper was purchased and while browsing through the news section, a face appeared that looked very familiar. It seems the motel guy blew away his wife with a handgun during some kind of confrontation. Makes one want to think of what could have happened, doesn't it?

BY THE NUMBERS

Before we were married, we talked about having children, and we spoke often about having a large family. But, who would have thought that there would be eleven? Nowadays, it seems, couples have children and then discuss it later. There was never any trouble in conceiving the little ones; each and every baby was a special event. Mike was born nine months after our marriage and all the family was in place by fourteen and a half years. The looks of amusement and amazement on the faces of strangers, as the brood was displayed in public, were fantastic.

ON THE FREEWAY TO OHIO

Traveling from military assignment to military assignment was always a logistical nightmare, especially later, as the numbers grew. Finding room for all the children in the cars was a challenge, let alone space for bags of clothes, diapers, diaper pails, or whatever. Travel was usually accomplished in a station wagon and a second car. On a couple of the later trips, walkie-talkies were employed so that potty breaks and meal breaks could be coordinated. Cellular phones were almost science fiction in those early days. On all the travels across the country, we sometimes got lost, but never were we separated.

In 1971, Dad had orders for duty in St. Louis, another move across the country, and another adventure. The sun was down and it was a little rainy as the family motored through downtown Kansas City. From out of the dark, comes a black and white police car and the patrolman starts to follow Mom in the station wagon with all the boys. He must have thought the sight was pretty amusing, because he proceeded to announce on his bullhorn, right there in traffic, "Where are the girls?"

Mom, without blinking an eye, pointed to Dave following in the little MG with our four-year-old, Theresa, waiving from her passenger seat. Mom had the last laugh on that one!

Christmas At The Mall

It was Christmas season, about '74 or '75, when we journeyed from our home at Edwards AFB to the San Bernardino Mall to do some shopping. The base was miles from anywhere with only the military exchange to shop at. We wanted the children to have the opportunity to look at all the toys and a chance to visit Santa. Malls were relatively new at the time so the trip was an event and a treat. The eight boys, all walking with Mom, were about fifty feet ahead of Dad and the three girls. A couple of older women (busybodies?) were noticed ahead, and they were proceeding towards us.

As they passed Mom and the boys, the whispered remarks began. "Did you see that poor mother?" "Imagine, eight boys!" "How does she cope?" "Poor thing!"

Dad's response, loud enough for everyone to hear as they passed our second group was, "And they were all planned, too!"

On The Trail

The Winnebago motor home was put to the test as the children were growing. One of the favorite haunts in the 70's was a campground in the High Sierras, not too far from Big Pine, California. It was a neat place as there was room for all the boys to pitch their two-man pup tents, while Mom and Dad could sleep in the Winnie with the little kids. The fishing was great. There were always trout in the creek and all the children became "hooked" on this sport; all are avid fishermen to this day. Day hikes were accomplished into the John Miur Wilderness and the family learned to appreciate the beauty of the woods and the outdoors.

It was either the summer of '75 or '76 when it was decided to take a longer trip, up the trail to include several overnights. A lot of planning went into this adventure. The older boys and Dad double packed and the little kids carried their own little pack. Mom brought up the rear on a horse with another packhorse and a guide to keep her out of trouble. To get a head start, everyone except Mom and the guide, hit the trail as the sun came up.

We were on the trail for about two hours when the family was met by three backpackers coming out. They looked pretty grubby but seemed to be in good spirits, as they were getting closer to home. As they passed us by we heard them question. "Wonder what scout troop that was?" We all thought that was pretty funny.

AMUSEMENT AND AMAZEMENT

From about our fourth little one on, a sense of awareness was felt as we took our children out in public. Carol usually had the boys dressed all alike, sometimes with clothes that she sewed herself. The boys all had burr haircuts until they were in high school. Again, Mom accomplished this task to save money and besides they looked good. One has to appreciate the picture of a brood, numbering anywhere from three or four to eleven children in tow, and they all looked so much alike that it was easy to tell they were one family.

One, again, has to imagine the look of panic on a restaurant manager's face as we entered asking for two high chairs, two youth chairs or boosters, and a table large enough for everyone! The manager usually solved this by reconfiguring a considerable portion of his restaurant. The children were usually quiet and undemanding in public. Mom and Dad were always proud as they noticed the looks of approval from the other patrons. Extra plates were requested so that meals could be shared, and of course, many glasses of milk would be ordered. The older boys would help the little ones with their meal and that was a large help. Milk spilled once in a while, but what can one expect? Quite often, one of the other customers would approach us as they were leaving and indicate what a nice and well-behaved family we had. Comments like that, needless to say, would always generate a warm feeling in us all.

We always made it a point to attend church on Sunday as a family (unless our little one was in the midst of the "terrible twos"). In that case, he or she was dropped at the nursery, so the congregation would not be disturbed. In later years, the family would take up an entire pew, that is, if the boys were not on the schedule to serve as altar boys. Again, a lot of looks and sideways glances were observed from others in church and many positive comments were always received after Mass. To this day, we still receive those comments from parishioners who remember the family at Mass years ago.

MOM'S SWEATSHIRT

Many years had passed. It was in the year 2005, specifically, that the story of Mom's sweatshirt took place. Martin and Lura, our fourth son and his wife, mailed Mom a sweatshirt for her birthday. But, this was no ordinary sweatshirt. On the front, they had figures embroidered representing our twenty-four grandchildren together with their names! The figures were arranged according to birth date from top right to bottom left. Across the top the title read "Grandma's Gang". Needless to say, the whole front of the garment was covered leaving only space for additional little ones on the back.

Mom received her gift just prior to our airline departure across the country. We were off to visit a couple of the kids and their families. Mom wore the shirt, of course, and from the very start of the trip, comments were received accompanied by all the usual questions. In the terminals, airplanes, restaurants, or even on the street, it was always the same. We had never visited with so many strangers before.

DIAPERS, DIAPERS, DIAPERS, AND ...

When you have babies, you have diapers; it is just part of the ball game. Nowadays, there exists what is commonly called "disposable diapers". Talk about "high tech". One just has to go to the store to purchase them and throw them in the garbage when they are dirty. Back in the old days with our brood, there was no such thing. We used cloth diapers.

NUMBERS AGAIN

The average age for our kids to be potty trained was about two and one-half years. Now, multiply that by 365 days, to find the number of days each kid was in diapers. A conservative number of diaper changes per day for each baby were nine, and there were eleven kids. One has to factor all this together in an equation to find how many diapers were changed overall.

$$2.5 \times 365 \times 9 \times 11 = 90,337.5 \text{ diapers}$$

We figured mathematically, that over the period of potty training for eleven we changed at least 90,338 diapers! It was probably good that the diapers were not of the disposable variety.

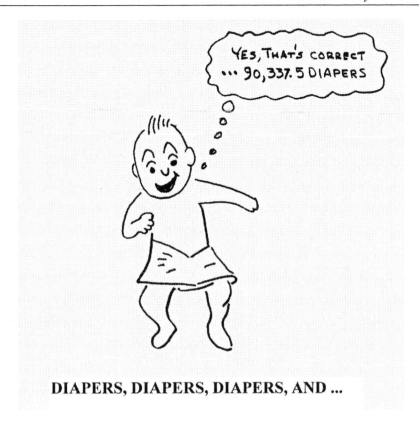

DIAPERS, DIAPERS, DIAPERS, AND ...

TECHNIQUE

Mothers seem to have that natural knack of doing all those things required in taking care of the little one, at least Carol did. Dave, on the other hand, had to acquire a certain amount of learning when it came to diaper changing, but he caught on fast. He had to.

He found it difficult to plug his nose for the dirty ones because it really took two hands to accomplish the diaper-changing task. The technique here was to breathe through the mouth. Carol taught him that running the sharp end of the diaper pin through his hair would facilitate pushing it through the cloth of the diaper. He also found by experience that having a second diaper close by to cover the vital parts during the critical exposure period would preclude him from becoming a target of opportunity.

Laundry

In reviewing the numbers game, one has to imagine the laundry chores, especially during the period when there were two or three little ones that were wearing diapers at one time. It seemed that the appliances were going full time, all the time, and we would rise several times at night, not only to check, feed, and change the little babies, but also to start another cycle of laundry. We often thought about sending the life cycle data on the washer and dryer to the manufacturers for their information and astonishment.

The first washing machine was purchased when Mike, the oldest, was born. At the time, we were living in a small upstairs apartment and, to compensate, the washer had to be crammed into the bathroom and set up to drain into the bathtub. Laredo, Texas was really hot. The diapers were transported outside to the clothesline, and by the time the last one was hung, the first would be dry enough to take down.

On a trip, the diaper logistical situation was solved with a diaper pail. The pail was always carried in the rear of the car and was emptied into the laundry upon arrival at home or at some other intermediate stop. Laundry always had a large priority.

Help

Coping with all the tasks was sometimes difficult just because of the numbers game and the limited time to do everything. The older boys were pressed into service when they were pretty young. Mike and Mark were changing dirty diapers from the time they were about age six. Mom and Dad just kind of closed their eyes as the boys would go after the baby with an open safety pin, but they didn't ever seem to stick them.

... MORE DIAPERS

No More Diapers

What a great day it was when the last one was finally "out of diapers." In later years, as the children (along with Mom and Dad) were experiencing the "terrible teens", we sometimes thought it would be nice if we were back changing diapers.

**"THE DIAPER PAIL WAS
INDISPENSABLE"**

LAUNDRY AND MORE

For most families, doing laundry is no big deal. For a family of eleven children, it was a primary concern. We couldn't let the dirty clothesbasket stand very long or it would overflow. The laundry and diaper pail were continually being dumped into the washing machine. The clean clothes would be pulled out and hung on the outside line or run through the dryer as soon as possible. Mom did most, but Dad or the kids helped out. Folding clothes became an evening ritual. Everyone understood what had to be done, but again Mom was the one who kept the handle on it and kept the whole show operating.

Hot Water

Dave received orders for Edwards Air Force Base in June of 1973. Carol was pregnant at the time and Michelle was born just a couple of weeks after moving into our government quarters. The laundry became even more important as we had eleven now with a couple in diapers.

Everything was pretty much "cool" except for one little "small problem". We were running out of hot water. We used cold water to wash the clothes and dishes. The big kids were taking cold showers and the little ones cold baths. A call was made to the base housing maintenance office and the folks came out to review our situation. The solution was to replace the water heater since it was relatively old. We thanked maintenance and continued on for a couple of days but again, the hot water would only last only for a short period of time, at best.

Another phone call was made to maintenance. This time, the supervisor arrived to check everything out. He instantly knew what the problem was when he saw all the kids running around and was informed that there were eleven. There was no way, he said, that the new heater could keep up with our family demands. It was simply too small. An industrial-sized water heater was promptly ordered and installed. The new heater, due to the size, had to be relocated in the kitchen broom closet because of the size and, of course, a certain amount of plumbing had to be accomplished for the new installation. We didn't have any hot water problems from that day on. We wonder sometimes if that same water heater or another of a similar size occupies the broom closet in the house we lived in so many years ago. Again, the great support we received as a military family has to be mentioned.

BY THE NUMBERS ... AGAIN

We had the laundry chore pretty much organized. But as the years passed, sorting the underwear became a problem. The kids were close enough together in age that the boys' briefs and t-shirts looked almost identical. The solution to this concern was to label them. Mom simply obtained a permanent black marker and inscribed a number on the waistband corresponding to the young lad as to where he stood in the stack. Mike, the oldest, was number one, Mark was number two, and so on down to Ted, number nine. Since we didn't have storage places for each individual, the underwear was placed in one or two drawers and the boys had to fish through all of it to find their own. You don't have to guess what Dad's number was. Yep! It was zero!

THROUGH THE YEARS

How can a simple task as laundry become such a large issue? The answer is simple: it was just a numbers thing. Organization, and not letting the daily tasks get away from us, was the solution. As we wrote in one of our Christmas letters to friends, years ago:

> *"The system is still working, although it is usually operating at full capacity. The system, if you haven't heard, is a master plan of coordinated effort running at maximum efficiency designed to accomplish all the mandatory tasks and related functions for normal family living."*

STITCHES AND BROKEN BONES

In every family of children, one usually has to go through the trauma of stitches and broken bones at some time or another. Our family was no different. All eleven had at least one cast for a broken limb and each had at least one visit to the emergency clinic for stitches. This, of course, was above and beyond the normal stuff like measles, chicken pox, mumps, common colds, and whatever else is out there to prey on the young. It's not the fact that we didn't or couldn't watch the kids close enough during play, games, or roughhouse, it's just that kids do not understand their own limitations or have enough experience to understand certain consequences. We were fortunate, when most of the children were young and going through this age, to have access to some fine military medical care. Some families didn't take well to the military clinics, but we found the medical personnel very professional and accommodating.

WAIT FOR THE CHANGE

We were stationed at Edwards Air Force Base from 1973 to 1978. Visits to the Air Force Clinic were so numerous that the Kerzie name became common among all the hospital staff.

The importance of always being on time was taught to all the children from an early age. To achieve this, the family would always rise early in order to accomplish some chores and make and bag lunches. Enough time was allotted so that everyone could rendezvous for their walk to school.

On one particular fine morning during this period, the kids were all demonstrating to each other how they could flip their milk money into the air and catch it in their mouth, and, you can readily guess what happened! Theresa, who was in the first or second grade at the time, swallowed her dime. Mom and Theresa were off to the hospital which, lucky for us, was only about a five-minute drive. As they entered the front door of emergency, the hospital commander, who just happened to be walking by, greeted her. "What is it this time, Mrs. Kerzie?"

Mom responded. "My daughter just swallowed a dime!"

The doctor, without batting an eye, replied. "Well, just take her home and wait for the change."

Theresa was checked, of course, with the x-rays and whatever else they do for kids that swallow stuff that isn't food. Afterwards, Theresa was taken home and it can be said that everything came out OK in the end.

GUNG HO

Todd, number eight, was attending Cal Poly University like all the others before and after him. The kids all shared one car but each had a bicycle to ride to and from the campus and their trailer home. On one particular fine spring day, Todd was racing from class to class on his bike and proceeded to "jet" across one of the campus roadways at full bore without checking for traffic. Again, you can guess what happened. Todd was bounced umpteen feet, much like that of a rubber ball after he was hit by an automobile traveling perpendicular to his path. Todd was very fortunate: only a broken leg. The bike was a disaster.

Todd was taken to the hospital, and surgery was performed later in the day to include placing a couple of steel pins in the joint that was fractured. Mom and Dad said a lot of prayers of asking and thanking during this trying period.

The doctor was making his rounds a couple of days later, when he asked Todd what he was going to do after graduation. Todd responded that he was in the U. S. Marine Corps Officer Candidate Program and that he really wanted to become a Marine Corps lieutenant. The doctor then proceeded to inform Todd that the Corps would not accept young men with pins in their legs.

Todd was a cross-country and long distance runner during his high school days. In fact, his school two-mile record held for about ten years. He is really a physical fitness enthusiast, and so, undeterred with the doc's and later, the military's criteria for commissioning, Todd started a physical self-therapy and reconditioning program. In about three months, his leg was back to almost normal strength whereupon he talked the doctor into a second surgery to remove the pins. Todd started all over with more therapy and conditioning, and a few months later he was able to pass the USMC Physical Fitness Test with flying colors.

Today, Todd is a career Marine officer and, so far, has held three commands. He is able to max out on his physical fitness test each time it is administered and is always able to out distance the Marines in his unit. Talk about "gung ho", but that is the USMC way.

CHESTER

Mark, the second oldest, was just getting through the terrible twos and was moving around extremely well for a little guy. Part of learning motor skills was climbing on furniture when Mom or Dad wasn't looking. One morning, he climbed one too many, slipped off one of the dining room chairs and sliced his leg at the knee joint.

Mom was again off to the base hospital emergency room and the corpsman was able to sew Mark up with more than a few stitches. The only trouble was that Mark, being the active one, kept bending his leg, and the wound was not healing properly. Mom called the clinic and they were able to coordinate a solution. Mom took an old magazine and cloth strips and made a splint for Mark's leg while leaving enough room for the wound to breathe. The real amusing part of the whole story was that it didn't slow Mark down one bit except he had to hobble around stiff legged. We nicknamed him Chester after one of the characters on TV's *Gunsmoke* at the time.

THROUGH THE YEARS

The family has been really fortunate with respect to good health. Matt ended up in intensive care twice when he was just a baby for pneumonia and Ted the same when he was only 6 months old. They looked so pathetic locked in their ice-cold breathing tents. Theresa had a kidney stone when she was college age and then she had problems a little later with ITP or thrombocytopenia, a not-too-well-known blood disease. The doctor blew away the stone with one of the new lithotripsy machines and the blood problem was taken care of by removing her spleen. Other than that, nothing serious has occurred with the children.

Many prayers of thanks have been said in regard to the health of our family. We have been so fortunate. Throughout their growing up, the children had been encouraged to participate in sports. We believe this fun-type physical conditioning has to promote healthy bodies as well as sound minds and a competitive spirit.

A DIARY OF LOST KIDS

No matter how careful parents are, kids can get lost. Tracking eleven is sometimes a problem.

"WE SOLD YOU THE HOUSE, NOT THE KID"

The time was November, of the year, 1966. There were Mom, Dad, and six boys (Mike 7, Mark 5, Matt 4, Martin 3, Thomas 2, and Timothy 1). Dad had just received orders for another move and so Mom sold the house to the mailman. Yes, that's correct: the mailman. So happy that we sold our neat little abode, that we agreed to let the buyers take possession early. With the closing complete, the household goods were packed and picked up for delivery and temporary quarters were assumed for six weeks in the basement of a downtown motel. At least the rooms were large, with enough beds for the boys, and the unit was warm for the cold South Dakota winter.

As we were taking one last look at our empty home, the new owners showed up with paint and other tools to do some remodeling. After explaining some of the house systems to the new owners, the kids were piled into the car for the motel. Bath time for all the boys came soon after arrival. We were bathing all the kids double or more but in configuring the bathtub something didn't add up. A kid was missing and his name was Tom. A search of the motel room was hastily accomplished but it didn't take long to realize Tom was really gone. His brothers couldn't remember Tom being in the station wagon during our trip to the motel. Could he have been left at the house? Naturally, the telephone had been disconnected and so Dad jumped in the car and drove back to our old home, probably breaking every speed law in town. Upon arrival, the un-assuming new owners and Thomas, having a field day running around an empty house, greeted Dad. The new owners were heard to respond. "We figured you would miss him sooner or later and would eventually come by to pick him up." Yes, the kid did not go with the sale of the house.

"WE SOLD YOU THE HOUSE ...
NOT THE KID!"

DAD'S MOST EMBARRASSING MOMENT

It was summer 1968, in Dayton, Ohio. We had Mom, Dad, Mike, Mark, Matthew, Martin, Thomas, Tim, and Theresa. It was a beautiful morning for the air show, especially after a hard rain the night before. Still a little cool, Mom dressed all the kids in their hooded sweatshirts. In order to keep things organized, Mom previously had sewed nametags on the front of each shirt. Theresa occupied the stroller with the diaper bag. She was only about age one at the time. Anyway, the show really started off great with all the airplanes doing flips, loops, and all. All the kids' attention was really riveted on the airplanes when someone noticed that Tom was missing. After a few minutes of searching the local area, and after the panic set in, three of the older boys were sent off in a search pattern to separate points of the compass. About this time an announcement was heard over the public address system to the effect that a lost little boy named Tom was being held at the Air Police tent and would his parents please come and claim him. All of us had a big sigh of relief. The Air Police tent was located down the airport ramp a couple of hundred yards. The tent was also located across a very large muddy field with some long boards put in place to facilitate as a walkway. Dad went running across the very muddy field, on a super-slippery walkway, post haste. You don't have to be a rocket scientist to imagine what happened next. About halfway across the before-mentioned field of mud, Dad, who is normally sure footed, slipped and fell flat on his face. He was covered with mud from head to toe, almost like in the movies. The embarrassing part of the whole story was that the entire episode took place in front of some stands filled with, what seemed like, several hundred spectators. The cheers were great. Yes, everyone knew who Tom's Dad was.

DAD'S MOST EMBARASSING MOMENT

Hey, Dad Bought One-too-many Cokes

The happy family was stationed at George AFB, Victorville, California, during the summer and fall of 1969. We had Mom, Dad, Mike, Mark, Matthew, Martin, Thomas, Timothy, Theresa, and Todd. Would you believe quarters was a very small three bedroom house on base, but it was only for six months and being a typical GI family, we made out. Needless to say, a lot of time was devoted to traveling and enjoying outdoor activities.

Victorville had a neat fairground and so when the county fair happened the family had to go. It was a typical hot hot day that only happens in the high desert. The fair was great with many exhibits and animals to look at. One interesting event was a little magic show, which caught the kid's attention. About this time, an announcement was heard on the public address that a horse race was about to take place. The kids were gathered and we headed for the fairground track. It was a great race and with the kids all being good, Mom and Dad decided to treat with cokes. Dad fetched the refreshments from the vendor stand but when passing them out came up with one too many. This couldn't be because Dad always knew how many kids he had and how many drinks to buy. He was right; we just didn't have enough kids. A quick head count revealed that Martin was missing, and for how long, was anyone's guess. The panic mode set in again and we started to back track our steps to the racetrack and then the magic show. We found Martin at the magic show with the biggest tears you ever saw. There were some tears of happiness and joy from the rest of us too. So much for the case of "One-Too-Many Cokes."

"Mary, Mary, Oh Mary, Where Have You Gone?"

It was summer of 1974 or 1975. We had Mom, Dad, Mike, Mark, Matt, Martin, Tom, Tim, Theresa, Todd, Ted, Mary, and Michelle. Michelle was only about one or two at the time so she occupied the stroller with the diaper bag. Mary was about three or four, had walked early, and was moving around extremely well for her age.

It was one fine weekend that we decided to hit the Los Angeles Zoo. An early arrival was accomplished and the whole day was devoted to looking at the various animals and exhibits. Mom had fixed sandwiches and we were able to have our picnic lunch in a nice grassy area. Toward sundown, we decided it was about time to head home, but on the way out, we stopped at the children's petting zoo. All the kids were good that day, undemanding and well behaved. It was then when we let our guard down. A final head count prior to leaving the park showed Mary missing. Talk about the gut wrench in the tummy as we searched the area for the next ten minutes. All of a sudden, she just showed up and not too concerned at that. We never did find out where she was. Maybe she was in the pen tending her sheep, (you know, like the nursery rhyme).

All Through The Years

One learns from experience and all through the years different techniques were developed which really helped in the organization and operation of the happy family. For instance, as we all departed in the Winnebago, whether from home plate or maybe some gas station on the way, Dad would call roll starting from Mike on down. As their names were called, the kids would reply with a healthy "here". All that was heard, when the roll call finally got down to Michelle, was a tiny dainty little response and everyone would laugh and giggle and we would be on our way for another adventure

LIFE AS A GYPSY FAMILY, OR, ON THE MOVE AGAIN

We moved no less than fourteen times during our first twenty years. This is the way for many families serving in the military service. It was always an adventure and an opportunity for us all to see and visit a new place.

How About The Children?

Would our kids be hurt by so many moves? How about the transition from one school to the next? Would they feel insecure moving from one domicile to another? Was there a psychological impact? These were just a couple of the questions we asked ourselves, as, we are sure, many others did in our situation (only we had up to eleven kids to be concerned about).

We found, through the years, that our kids could really adapt. It was tough for them, as they grew older, to leave their friends but they learned to make new ones quickly. Some of our kids still correspond or keep in contact with friends they made when they were in elementary or high school. The ability to make friends easily was, maybe, a result as their life as gypsies.

We tried to shift the odds in their favor by shopping for good schools at our new destination before settling on a place to live.

The curriculums varied somewhat from one portion of the country to another but the kids always scrambled to catch up if they were deficient in a particular area. We found that if we carefully monitored their progress and acted appropriately that they wouldn't be put in a position from which they couldn't recover. The younger children had a more stable environment with respect to their education as they lived in the same location. Do we detect a difference between our older children and the younger kids in their learning? Not really. Maybe our experience would be a good case study for some aspiring educator.

THE MOVE

It became easier each time we made a move because we learned from the experiences of the previous ones. Or, maybe it was more difficult, with each move, as we often had an additional baby or two. We learned to look ahead in our packing and how to coordinate with the moving people. For example, essentials that were required for our road trip and those items to hold us over until our household goods arrived at the destination were put in a separate box in the corner so that the movers wouldn't throw them on the van. During the packing operation, the packers would place inventory stickers on each piece of furniture or box. The little kids thought it was great sport to remove these stickers and attach them to another piece or box unknowingly creating a great amount of confusion. The children also had great fun making forts or houses from the many packing boxes stationed around our home. This all created an increased demand on Mom and Dad's part to keep things in order. Formed bed sheets were fitted to each mattress so that we wouldn't have to search through the numerous boxes that would pile up at the destination. It usually took the movers two days to pack and one day to load the van. We always asked that the washing machine, clothes dryer, and playpen went on the van last so that they would come off first at the destination. Some of the tasks were unusual for the packers at our home. A good example was the requirement to disassemble four sets of bunk beds. But they always were able to cope. We found the movers that the government contracted with were very professional and accommodating. At our destination, it was always a treat for the kids to see their toys unpacked, almost like Christmas again.

A HOME TO LIVE IN

Sometimes we rented a house, and other times, a home was purchased and then sold when orders were received for the next assignment. We lived in military housing when it was available and when those quarters were large enough for our expanding family. The trauma of buying a home never became routine as we were usually scrounging for the cash to make a down payment. The rent for our first apartment was $40 per month and the mortgage payment on our first home was $115 a month. But back then, that was a significant portion of Dave's military pay. Later, with all the children, we always attempted to find a home with a large enough dining room to facilitate our large table. Bedroom space was also given a high priority and the boys learned early about bunk beds and bunkrooms. An open stairway, often found in a two-story home, was a no-no for Carol. She always had visions of one of the kids doing a somersault or half gainer from the upstairs to the first deck. A large yard was always nice as the family spent a lot of time outdoors. In any case, we always found ways to accommodate.

THROUGH THE YEARS

We often reminisce about the times we experienced as a gypsy family. Would we do it over again? You bet we would! Sure, pulling stakes every couple of years was a hardship, but we really had a lot of fun at the same time.

THE EVENING MEAL

Some call the evening meal a "dinner"; others call it "supper". In our home, it was always "dinner", and it was an event that all members of the family made a point to attend. It was a time when everyone could share the experiences of their day. More importantly, it was a special time when the family members would get together to bond. Imagine a dinner table set for thirteen, every evening.

THE EARLY YEARS

The evening meal was a family occasion even from when the first baby was born. Little Mike would sit in his baby-bouncing chair, either on the table or on the dining room floor if the temperature permitted. If he hadn't been fed his bottle as yet, Mom was able to do that by cradling him in her left arm, holding the bottle with her left hand, while at the same time eating her own dinner with her right. It was only a few weeks after our babies were born when Carol would start them on baby food and cereal. The baby food didn't seem too appetizing to Dave but the little babies devoured it all. If they didn't like one particular flavor, it would immediately be spit out all over their bib.

As more babies came along and as they grew older, the configuration of the dining room changed. The children would graduate from the bouncing chair to a high chair, then to a youth chair, and finally, to a regular chair, maybe with a cushion or pillow. At one time, we had a bouncing chair, one high chair, and four youth chairs. But, the newest little one would always have his or her place at (or on) the dining table. Eventually, the happy family finally ended up with a table that would extend and enough chairs to seat fourteen adults.

DINNER

We always started dinner with a prayer of thanksgiving, and the little ones, from almost the time they could talk, would take their turn at saying grace. Once into the meal, conversation sometimes got a little unwieldy and Dad would have to exercise control to make things return to normal. One of the methods, among others, was to assign a current event from the daily newspaper to one of the kids. He or she would then present what was read to the family for discussion. That idea, although it didn't last too long, seemed to keep the conversation to a low roar. The lessons learned over the years, however, included that one had to be courteous and not interrupt.

THE LATER YEARS

In the later years, when the children became involved with activities, we still made an attempt to schedule dinner at as close to the regular time when everyone could be present. Years later, when the children were older and could help themselves; the meal would be served mess hall style from the kitchen stove or kitchen island. Mom would fix one of her standard meals, no special menus for individuals. Sunday was always special and quite often we would have guests for dinner. Card tables and chairs were set up if more seats were needed.

LOOKING BACK

Our fourth oldest is a dentist in Pennsylvania. Martin asked one of his office people one day why the young lad seemed to have a strong and happy family experience. His response was that his family ate dinner together every evening.

We strongly believe, that being able to rendezvous the family together at some point of the day really helps cement the strength of the unit. A great opportunity is the evening meal. Is this an impossible task in today's environment of school activities, sports, scouts, working mothers, or whatever?

One needs to set the priorities: What is most important?

DISCIPLINE

Our parents were descendants of "old" European culture. Dave's Grandparents were Slovenian and Norwegian; Carol's were German and Irish. Children of their age were seen and not heard. Children had respect for their elders, and strict discipline was the norm of everyday life for children.

As we were growing up, our parents disciplined us in a similar manner but probably not as harsh as in their own upbringing. Carol, more than once felt the spanking hand of her father across her behind, while Dave felt it on his butt through the smack of his father's bedroom slipper. We both had the "stand in the corner routine" and, of course, the denial of treats that we would have normally enjoyed. Our mothers were just as strong in their methods of discipline but in a little softer manner. We were never able to play one parent against the other; they were always united in what they passed out or taught. Whatever the case, on looking back, we deserved what we received. Our parents were always fair with their just punishments. The following paragraphs reflect some of our own ideas on discipline in the family and how we implemented them.

As the years pass, a certain amount of a more permissive society has been noticed. Is this a product of the way children are being raised? Books (and more books) have been written on child discipline and how to raise children. We believe that kids will push their parents just to see how far they can get or how much they can get away with.

We have seen some two-year-olds that are in complete control of their parents.

Children are never too young to learn consideration for others, and this includes respect for parents and other elders. We believe that if the parents placed emphasis on this at a child's early age that it would be an easier task downstream to discipline later. If a young person has respect for his or her elders, then he or she will pay attention to and understand better the teachings of morals and values. Important, also, is the example set by parents. We learned from observing others early on that the children will imitate Mom and Dad. If Mom and Dad are screamers, then the children will become screamers. If Mom or Dad is a whiner, then the children will tend to whine. If Mom and Dad are cool or mellow, then the children, as a general rule, will act the same.

Teaching children self-discipline is another aspect of rearing children, which is so important. And again, if the parents show a lack of self-discipline, what can one expect from the offspring?

We tried to emulate our parents in the way we disciplined all our children. Yet, our methods would change somewhat depending on each individual child's behavior and personality. Still, an attempt to be as consistent as possible, concerning discipline among all the children, was important to us. We learned a tremendous amount from our experience and made an attempt to capitalize on it as the years passed. Dave's problem was his lack of patience. This was somewhat balanced out by Carol's complete cool but firm demeanor under fire. We worked together as a team. There was no pleading or negotiations with the children on the part of Mom and Dad. There was no "Please?" when the children were told, not asked, to behave. The kids were made to clearly understand why they were being corrected. Discussion occurred in some instances, especially when the children became older, but only in a civil manner. "Talking back" was not tolerated and an absolute no-no. "Time outs" sometimes reminds one of a ballgame or sporting event, almost a piece of cake for being out of order. We felt the children must learn the consequences of misbehaving or causing trouble. If this required a spanking, then it happened. But, this was a last resort, well thought out, and not a release of our frustrations. If one tends to threaten with some form of discipline, then one has to follow through and we adhered to that principle the best we could. We feel that one of the most important aspects of discipline is to be fair and we made an attempt to do this across the board. We treated discipline as a very serious matter.

Discipline was administered not only when kids were misbehaving, but also at good times, through communication about morals and any other topic which makes a young person think about being a good citizen. This was accomplished sometimes at the dinner table when at least once a day all the family could be gathered together, or, maybe, sometimes while riding in the car, or, maybe, around a campfire. It was not always as a family that these conversations took place, but sometimes one- on-one or one-on-two if the occasion presented itself. The children, from the time they were in the first grade, were required to attend church school in addition to their normal school, so as to receive views from others on how to act in society and as a family member.

Were we strict because of our methods of discipline? Probably yes. Were we politically correct by today's standards in the way we disciplined our children? Probably not. Parents nowadays are being sued for not giving their children equal rights. But, if we had to do it all over again, we wouldn't change a thing.

THE ANIMALS

For about the first eighteen years, our family didn't have any pets. It wasn't that animals were not liked; it was just not logistically possible with all the children and all the moves that were part of being a military family. Towards the last part of our military career, and from then on though, things began to change.

HEIDI

It was 1977, during the last part of our assignment at Edwards Air Force Base, when our family fell in love with Heidi. She was a Saint Bernard puppy and was one of a litter given to us by one of our good neighbors. Heidi was like a little fuzz ball and was really cute. It didn't take long though for Heidi to grow into her big feet. Heidi was very gentle around the children but at the same time very protective. For instance, when the children would start playing on the backyard block fence, Heidi would become very nervous, start barking, and would not let up until she thought the kids were safe on the ground.

Heidi grew up with the kids. She turned out to be very massive in size. If you recall seeing the Saints standing at attention in the snows of the Swiss Alps, with the barrel hanging from their neck, then you can picture Heidi. She loved the winter and would run around the back yard, tossing snow all over the place, just like a little kid.

It was about three years after Heidi became a family member that she became the center of a most embarrassing moment. The occasion was when Carol, with eight of the youngest and Heidi, traveled from Ohio by airline, to meet Dave and the three oldest in California. This was the one time when it was decided, for several reasons, that it was best to travel by air. As you know, animals have to travel in a special compartment in their own container on the airplane. To make matters worse, the trip's itinerary included a stop and airplane switch in Chicago. To say the least, Heidi was really happy to see us when they unloaded the animals at the Los Angeles terminal.

The main reason she was happy though, was that she had to go potty. We didn't think too much about her situation, as everyone was so happy to see each other. When we arrived outside the terminal, Heidi started to tug on her leash, but didn't know what to do, because all that was around were thousands of people and acres of concrete. Heidi finally couldn't stand it any longer, took her squat right in the middle of LAX, and cut loose. Talk about a fire hose. All the pedestrians and airline folks thought it was really funny. We were embarrassed and Heidi was much relieved.

THE SNAKE WHO THOUGHT HE WAS AN ESCAPE ARTIST

It was the year 1980, when we finally settled in Palmdale, California. All the kids were in school, from second year in college to first grade. Youngest son Ted was pretty well underway in his studies at elementary school. His teacher at the time had a gopher snake as a classroom pet and nature project. The snake was kept in an aquarium and Ted's classmates became pretty good friends with it. Summer vacation came along and Ted's teacher asked if the family would baby sit the snake for a couple of months. Of course, the kids insisted, and so, the snake became a temporary fixture in our home.

When school resumed in the fall, the snake assumed its place back in the classroom. This time however, a couple of the new parents objected to the snake occupying the same room as their children.

You know it! The snake became a permanent resident of the Kerzie home.

Permanent is a vague term sometimes. Although a cover was secured to the top of the snake's cage, he somehow got loose. Everyone looked all over for several days before he was found curled up in a very cramped area between the hallway cupboard and the wall. It took a lot of patience and ingenuity to coax him out but, with the aid of a hair dryer and a bent clothes hanger, the feat was finally accomplished. Dad stated in a rather firm manner. "Don't let him out again," and so, proper precautions were made.

That is what everyone thought. Several months later, the snake escaped again. Where did he go this time? We looked high and low, but no joy. It was about three weeks later when Mom's folks came to visit. Grandpa and Grandma were given the bed in the master bedroom while Dad and Mom slept in the camper. One day, when Grandpa was walking down the hallway, he spied the empty cage and asked what it was for. Mom's response was that it wasn't really anything and passed it off like there was nothing wrong. It was after the grandparents had departed for back home and Mom and Dad were in the bedroom changing the sheets when we noticed the cat sniffing around the bed.

Dad exclaimed. "I wonder?"

The mattress was pulled off of the bedsprings and there was the lost snake! It was coiled all up in the box springs and had obviously found a quiet, dark, and temperature-pleasing place to hibernate. Grandpa and Grandma were never told that they had been sleeping on a snake for a week.

The snake was kept for years in our home. There was a certain amount of mixed reactions from all our visitors when they viewed the snake. Visitors were sometimes warned, and sometimes, not just to see the various reactions. Ted finally claimed ownership a couple of years ago and the snake now happily feeds on pet store rodents at Ted's home with Ted and Ted's bride, Tiff.

TOM'S NERF

Tom, like many of his brothers and sisters, worked part time at Sear's Veterinary Hospital for part-time employment. They did this while attending high school and college. Our family owes Dr. Sears and his wife for helping our children as they struggled through the "halls of higher learning". Anyhow, Tom arrived early for work one Saturday morning during the summer to open up. As he approached the front door, he found a little Black Lab puppy tied to a bush along with a bag of dog food. Obviously, someone had abandoned this poor little pup. Tom immediately fell in love with the Lab, and also knew that the vet would have to take the dog to the pound if no one laid claim. Tom begged Mom and Dad and so we ended up with another animal. We named him Nerf.

It's funny how animals will attach themselves to a certain human. Nerf became especially attached to Mom. All our dogs were outside dogs, but as Nerf became older, we took pity and he was let into the house. It was fun to watch Nerf follow Mom, as she would traverse her course around the home cleaning or doing the chores.

CRICKET

This is a story of probably the saddest day of our family concerning animals. We were stationed at Edwards AFB between 1973 and 1978. The quarters on base were somewhat cramped, and therefore, the family spent quite a bit of time out of doors. The weather was nice most of the year and Dad and the boys devoted many hours in the garage, working on projects like building model airplanes and lamps. It was during this time that an enormous-sized cat started showing up and would spend a considerable amount of time with us. He would jump up on one of the workbenches, lie down, and just watch. We found out soon after that he belonged to some neighbors down the street and that his name was Cricket. The neighbors didn't seem to care and Cricket kind of adopted our family.

This cat was the king of the neighborhood. First of all, he was a very large cat, almost like a dog with very fluffy hair. He was also very independent and did what he wanted to do. When our neighbors were reassigned, the cat became ours free and clear and I guess that was OK with Cricket. It sure was with the kids!

About a year later, orders were received for another move to Ohio. What do we do with Cricket? We knew cats were very territorial and do not take very well to moves especially after they have been established. We consulted with the vet and he recommended we give it a try and prescribed some medicine to help with the cross-country trip.

All our cross-country trips were an adventure and this one was no different. Can you imagine a motor home, a second car, eleven kids, a St. Bernard and a cat, all trying to make their way together from California to Ohio without incident? Dad had spent a couple of months at his new assignment in Ohio, already purchased a house, and so we thought everything was pretty much greased. The crew that picked up the household goods in California told us Dad was planning a house-to-house move, and if we hurried, we would have our furniture soon after we arrived. With that understanding, we departed almost immediately and the drive across the country was accomplished in minimum time.

We moved into our new home with only what we had in our car. We were used to being a GI family and could cope with situations like this. After about a week though, we began to wonder where our "stuff" was, and Dad finally called the base traffic management office. After a little research, they explained that the moving van driver decided to take a vacation, was on the East Coast, and would be at our home to deliver in about another week! Mom was telephoned with the bad news but before Dad could speak, Mom began to relate something much worse. It seems Mike, the oldest, wrecked the front end of the car while dumping some rubbish from the yard. To continue the sad story, Dad rushed home to collect the car with the bashed front, found it would run, and limped home. Everyone was upset to say the least. Dad wanted to put the car in the garage but the Winnebago was blocking the driveway. Dad, in his somewhat uncool state, jumped into the camper, started it up to move it, threw it into reverse, and ran over Cricket.

In the week that we had been in our new home, Cricket was finally becoming acclimatized to his new environment. Still, the camper must have been a familiar surrounding and he was evidently hiding behind the wheel. Part of the sadness was that all the kids, including some new neighbor friends, witnessed the whole incident. It wasn't a very good day.

Biggens Went Awol

Biggens was one of several cats that we had in our family. Biggens was an unassuming cat but always seemed to have a lot of fun with the kids. He liked to sit on a stool in the middle of the room and intercept a paper ball or whatever the kids might be playing catch with. He would do this for hours without losing interest.

One day during the summer, Biggens disappeared. We looked for him all over but he was long gone. We knew he didn't run away because he was a close family pet. He had been missing for almost a month when all of a sudden, he showed up. Dad was out in the front yard doing chores when Biggens trotted down the driveway. He really looked happy! He took about three laps around the house just to make sure everything was the same and then wouldn't let us out of his sight. We wished he could talk to us to let us know what had happened or where he had been. We think that he may have gotten trapped in one of the neighbor's sheds or maybe in the frame of a car or our motor home and was transported somewhere far away before he could free himself. Anyhow, Biggens went AWOL, and we were sure happy he found the way home.

ALL THE ANIMALS

The younger children had more of an advantage when it came to growing up with animals. It was good in the fact that they learned responsibility in taking care of their pets. At one time we had a pony, three dogs, three cats, twenty-five chickens, two rabbits, a snake, and a tarantula spider. Seemed more like a zoo, but it was great!

NICKNAMES

It seems that kids always come up with nicknames ... and ours were no different. Most of the children just had shortened versions of their given name ... like Michael was Mike and Matthew was, of course, Matt. Some of the names were different however and had no semblance to their given name. Theresa, because she was the first girl born after six boys was nicknamed "Gal". This name was laid on her from the time she was almost a baby. Today she is known as "Gal", even though she is a young mother herself. Michelle was called "Neb" (for some reason) from the time she was in elementary school. We believe Matt was the one that gave her that one and it stuck. Years later, when she was playing varsity basketball for Cal Poly University, one could hear from the stands a "Come on, Neb!"

As soon as the numbers stabilized, the children divided themselves into "little pigs" and "big pigs." Why this happened is unknown, except that the kids generated the "pig thing" and it generally had to do with chores, or, maybe it had to do with, "It's time to go to bed." Quite often, the big pigs were permitted to stay up to study or to do homework for school. When an older one left home more or less on their own, a "little pig" would have the dubious honor of graduating to the ranks of the "big pigs." This probably meant, for example, that instead of being in rotation for clearing the dining table that he or she would be mowing or weeding the lawn or garden.

HAIL, FAREWELLS, AND SEPARATIONS

Dave was commissioned as an Air Force lieutenant a couple of weeks before our marriage. The fact that being away from one's spouse for extended periods of time was a norm for a military family was soon readily confirmed. We had discussed all the ramifications of being away from home and the traumas of being separated, but we strongly believed that we could cope.

Our parents were somewhat apprehensive and felt that we were too young for marriage. On the other hand, we had been romancing each other for three years and to wait any longer, especially with Dave having orders in hand, would be unbearable for us both.

The temporary duties (TDY's) and alert tours away from the family occurred very frequently during Dave's twenty-year military career. Some were only three or four days but many lasted three or four weeks. The longest was six months, in support of the Vietnam conflict, and then there was Dave's yearlong assignment to Vietnam (in country). Was it the roll of the dice? We never missed a Christmas those twenty military years but we never had a wedding anniversary together either. Carol, with the kids at home, would take over the role as Dad when Dave packed his bags and departed. She learned plumbing, auto mechanics, yard work, and all those chores that Dad would normally take care of. The children were great at helping out and probably matured earlier with respect to assuming responsibilities than most.

THE BIG FAREWELL

It was Christmas season of 1969. There was Mike, Mark, Matt, Martin, Tom, Tim, Theresa, and Todd. During the previous six months, the family lived at George AFB California where Dave was assigned for training. At graduation, the orders read Phu Cat Air Base Vietnam and the normal length for this remote assignment was one year. The troops were not receiving a short tour unless, of course, they were casualties. Dave had volunteered for this assignment and was looking forward to the flying. We were not looking forward to a year apart, though, having experienced some long separations before.

It was an easy decision to move the family to Salina, Kansas, where the Army had set up a base for those loved ones whose husbands and Dads were sent to Southeast Asia. This was a good deal as the Army took good care of those "lost families". We were able to drive from George to Salina, get settled in the new house, and enjoy the Christmas holidays before Dave's departure, but all the time we were consciously (but silently) counting the days.

The fateful day arrived and we all piled into the station wagon for the short journey to Kansas City. Dave had his commercial airline flight scheduled from there to his port of U.S. departure. We didn't say a whole lot during the trip to Kansas City but only discussed last minute items. The children were unusually quiet. It started to snow as we pulled into the airport terminal and we thought it best just to say our good-byes there at the curb. Talk about a gut wrench in the tummy. The older kids, those that knew what was going on, started to cry. Todd, our baby at 14 months, all of sudden started to jabber baby talk and everyone started laughing and crying at the same time. It sure was a lonesome feeling as Dad watched the station wagon start down the road with all the kids peering out the windows for that one last look.

THE LONG SEPARATION AND BABY TED

The first couple of months in Vietnam went quickly for Dave as he was learning the new mission and finishing his familiarization as a "new guy". Then as things became more routine, the time started to drag, and thoughts of those at home caused a considerable amount of loneliness. Being a member of a fighter squadron seemed to help, as all the guys were first class. Back home, Carol was kept busy with the kids' schools and multitude of activities, which the Army had set up. There were Scouts, Little League, church activities, you name it. The older boys kept up their airplane model building and so there were contests to attend. Trips were made to Kansas City to watch big league ball games. It was important for everyone to keep active.

One has to remember that the year was 1970. Worldwide communications via satellite were unheard of. Long distance telephone was primitive from Vietnam and we were able to talk by phone only twice during the year. E-mail? What is that? And so, letter writing remained for us the only means of getting together. We were good about writing each other and we always found time each day to do that. What a great day it was when a letter or two was found in the mailbox. The snapshots were a special treat.

Of course, Carol was pregnant when Dave departed and so there was one more little problem to work out. The little one was due in June, about six months into Dave's tour. Carol had a baby sitter set up for when she had to go to the hospital for delivery. Imagine what Dave was going through thousands of miles away.

It was close to delivery time when Dave contacted the MARS station on base. MARS was the local Military Amateur Radio Station set-up that Dave had become aware of by talking to his buddies. A phone call was placed to the GI's manning the station and they promised to help. Dave then went to bed but was awakened by his phone a couple of hours later. The troops in the MARS station had established contact with a ham in the states and an in-country phone patch was in progress! The baby sitter answered, "Carol is in the hospital, call back later!" What a coincidence! After the connection broke, Dave convinced the MARS operators to try a few hours later. What a bunch of neat guys! Contact was again established and, this time, the ham operator in the U.S. was able to patch directly into Carol's recovery room. We were able to talk for just a couple of minutes, but what an experience. The baby was a boy and his name was Ted. Both Mother and baby were doing well and everything was cool! By the way, Dave was notified a week later by the Red Cross that again he was a father.

THE LONG TRIP HOME

Dave was granted a roll back that curtailed his yearlong tour by two weeks. He was going to be home for Christmas!

He was able to catch a hop out of Phu Cat to Cam Rahn Bay Air Base and then the "Freedom Bird" through Japan to Seattle. An airline ticket was in hand for a United Airlines flight to Salt Lake City with a subsequent Frontier Airline connection to Salina, less than a mile from Carol and the kids. But, even the best laid plans go astray. United was late departing Seattle. Dave was on the edge of his seat all the way to Salt Lake, knowing that it was going to be close for his connection. As soon as his plane landed, Dave hit the ramp running, only to catch sight of the Frontier flight as it was leaving the gate. What a letdown! The next flight to Salina was not for twenty-four hours. After a year away, do you believe another day would make a difference? You bet it did! A ticket was purchased for Wichita and Carol and the kids picked Dad up at 2AM after a two-hour drive. Was it all worth it? What a dumb question!

WHITE MARBLES
AND BLACK MARBLES

It was tradition in our family to have a nice family dinner on Sunday. We felt it important to rendezvous for family dinner every day but Sunday was always special. Quite often, we would ask Father Steve over, and more often than not, he would accept.

As the boys became older and started dating, it became a ritual to invite the girlfriends over for the Sunday affair. We always had a large dining table to accommodate everyone and so a few more didn't make any difference. Mom did a great job cooking for fifteen or twenty. Do you think the girls, the kids' dates, might be a little intimidated? Imagine a young lady anticipating an appraisal from her guy's family of ten siblings plus Mom and Dad!

We used to joke about those situations and the boys in their sometimes "sick humor" would talk about white marbles and black marbles. Meaning, after the young date left for the evening, a bowl would be passed around and each one would drop in a marble of what they thought was the appropriate color. This was a made-up story, of course, but the kids had a lot of fun telling it among themselves.

But, the marble thing almost backfired. Matthew had graduated from the university and was carrying on the merry life of a bachelor in San Diego. Matt called home one week and mentioned that he had met a real nice girl and would like to bring her up for a weekend to meet the family. Her name was Jackie. The only thing was that Matt, with his big mouth, told Jackie the "marble story", and he didn't mention that it was all fiction. Anyhow, Matt and Jackie started for home, Jackie got sick about halfway, barfed beside the side of Interstate 15 and they promptly turned around and motored back to San Diego. Was she nervous to the point of getting sick with anticipation? Probably.

Matt and Jackie tried it again a couple of weeks later. This time they made it all the way. Visitors and friends were always made welcome in our home and the young ladies and young men that ours were courting felt like part of the family after only a few minutes. We all fell in love with Jackie that weekend and I think she did with us. She said later, though, that she was a nervous wreck as she and Matt were walking to the front door that first time. Matt and Jackie were married about a year later and are living happily ever after.

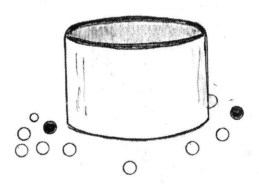

POTPOURRI

CHRISTMAS '66

Military orders read for assignment to Edwards Air Force Base and so the family packed for the trip cross country, to the sunny skies of Southern California. Our roster consisted of six boys by this time. This was December of 1966 and winter travel through portions of South Dakota, Wyoming, Utah, and Nevada had to be carefully thought out. Tire chains were loaded in the trunk of each car for easy access in case of need and the weather forecasts were thoroughly reviewed.

Departure was accomplished from Rapid City a few days before Christmas with the hopes that Santa might find us in California. The first day out, found Mom and five of the boys in the lead car, traveling the barren highways of desolate Wyoming. The temperature was well below freezing and the wind was blowing at a good forty knots. Dad with the remaining boy in the MGA was close in trail when, you guessed it, the left rear tire blew. Mom wasn't watching the mirror too closely, but finally, got the idea something was wrong when after a few miles a cross check revealed no one following. Dad already had the rear jacked up by the time she arrived back on the scene. If you have never changed a tire in chill factors like this, you don't know what you have missed!

To complicate the situation, about this time was that the kids were starting to get sick, each with a case of the flu. You know what happens with flu: Besides feeling awful, you throw up! Provisions were made with plastic buckets and one really had to feel sorry for the poor little guys as the ravages of the flu made its way from one little one to the next.

A couple of days later found us in Provo, Utah. This was Christmas Eve. The boys were still not well, the weather was crummy, the planned time line was shot, and so the decision was made to spend our Christmas Eve in a motel. After the family was settled, Dad went out to fetch McDonald's hamburgers and cokes for those who could eat. Makes one think of the adventures of Mary and Joseph in Bethlehem.

About two in the morning, Dad awoke and silently crept out to the car where Christmas presents were hidden under the seats. Together with Mom, the gifts were all laid out under a little tiny tree in the corner of the motel room. You should have seen the kids light up in the morning. One could say that it was a moment that Dad and Mom will never forget. Makes it all worth it, doesn't it?

THE RAILROAD BRIDGE

One of the neat places we used to go camping at during the seventies and the eighties was San Onfre Beach. The campground was located on Camp Pendleton Marine Corps Station, not too far from San Diego. We were able to park the old Winnebago almost on the water and the kids had room to pitch their pup tents near the sand. The drive to the beach was no more than three hours so that weekend trips were feasible.

The story of the railroad bridge takes place during the summer of 1985. Not all the kids were with us on this particular trip, as two were already married and living back east, while others were off at school. Father Steve, our adopted Catholic priest friend, came down to join us for a short vacation away from the trials and tribulations of his parish. This story would not be complete without Father Steve.

About mid-day, little Mary got caught up in an undertow while surfing. Father saved her "little behind" by diving in the ocean and dragging her to the shore. By the time Dave got to them, both were lying on the sand, exhausted. Father Steve was the hero for the day until later that afternoon.

Father Steve happens to be a big railroad fan. Big full-size ones or models: It makes no difference. It happens that railroad tracks are located only about a mile or so from the beach and our campground. This is the line on which Amtrak makes its regular runs. Father Steve took Theresa, Todd, Ted, Mary, and Michelle for a short hike, and of course, the walk gravitated towards the railroad tracks. They all get the big idea to cross the trestle, which was probably not good because there was no way to get off except at the ends.

You know what happened next. About halfway across, they hear the whistle. They couldn't jump because of the height and so they took off running. Father Steve brought up the rear pushing the last little one who happened to be Theresa. It was obvious that Father and Gal were not going to make it before the train got to them. Father grabbed Gal and they hugged the side of the bridge as close as they could with the Amtrak train whistling by, at however many miles an hour it travels, within inches of their nose. Imagine the terror on the bridge! Imagine the terror in the rest of the kids as they were counting heads and wondering what happened to Gal and Father as the train went roaring past!

Father Steve swore the kids to secrecy. "Don't tell your mom and dad about this!" The secret was kept for years, only to be let out by Mary. Her school assignment one semester was to write about her most terrifying moment. Evidently, she didn't think it would get back to Mom and Dad, and besides, it was a great story! On reflecting back to that time long ago, the Lord sure must have been with us that day.

WINNEBAGO STORIES

Input from everyone

Our family's trusted Winnebago "home on wheels" has gone to motor home heaven. Whether our family trip was to a model contest, the beach, Big Pine, up the coast, or wherever, "the camper" would always get us there safely and provide us shelter from the elements. Many of our growing up experiences transpired while vacationing in our home-away-from-home. The family was queried to come up with a list of "camper memories" from the twenty-five years the Winnebago was part of our family. Here is what was gathered. Remember when...

Mom and Dad used to swap drivers without stopping the camper.

Ted fell off the bunk bed at Big Pine and busted his head wide open.

Dad drove under a low under-pass in Seattle and knocked the model airplane boxes off the top of the camper, and Mike and Mark spent the next forty-eight hours scrambling to get their models rebuilt for the contest.

Someone would forget to lock the fridge and when Dad would turn a corner all the sodas and food would fall out, on one of the six people sleeping on the floor.

We all slept in that thing in the church parking lot at Lake Elsinore when it was pouring down rain.

We had the flat on Interstate 5 in the middle of nowhere. We kept ourselves amused watching a crop duster while Dad, Mike, and Mark changed the tire.

Dad ran over Cricket, the cat. That was the day Mike crashed the station wagon. What a sad day.

Mom and Dad made us wash and wax the sucker.

We watched Planet of the Apes *on the little portable TV while driving to a model contest in Fresno.*

We would go somewhere and one of us always had to shout, "I CALL THE FRONT SEAT WITH MOM!"

Or, sit on the hump between the two front seats, because it was the warmest place on the way to church.

We lived in it for two weeks waiting for our house in Palmdale to get built.

Didn't Dad and Mark live in it for nine months while Mom tried to sell the house in Beavercreek?

Dad had to stop on the freeway outside of Bakersfield because he could not see ten feet ahead. We were in the middle of a huge sandstorm. It took two weeks to get all that desert dust out!

We always camped at space #1 at Big Pine.

Mike and Mark had to help Dad dump the sewage after camping. That's when a little pig was glad to be a little pig!

The big pigs had to sleep in those orange two-man tents. Again, that's when a little pig was glad to be a little pig.

We played the license plate game (first one to get to ten or all the ABCs) just to pass the time.

On our way to Oregon, we had to slow down because we saw a bear crossing the road.

We used to fall asleep on the hot floor of the camper while Dad was driving.

When he hit the dirt road, we all knew we were almost home, and wished he would keep driving around the block so we could keep sleeping.

We went to a model contest at Taft in the middle of August, a couple weeks after Michelle was born. The A/C broke and it was a good 105 degrees. All the kids were covered with layers of sand and airplane guck. We went into park restrooms and cleaned up for church.

We used to drive the Winnie to church every Sunday because it was the only vehicle we could fit in.

Those were some really great times!!

"THOSE WERE SOME REALLY GREAT TIMES"

EXPRESSIONS OF LOVE

Input from Theresa

DAD'S NOTES

As parents, we were so fortunate to have children who were capable of expressing their love. Some were more "touchy feel" or physical; others would better express their affection through a deed or event. Much of the children's physical affection was spontaneous even from when they were the smallest babies. In addition, as the children grew older, notes, letters, and other projects would arrive with expressed feelings and thoughts which were really so genuine that one knew that they had to be generated from the heart, and they would generate a tear or two on Mom and Dad's part.

Back in 1978, Theresa was in the fifth grade. The Woman's Club on the base nominated, as an annual event, a "Mother of the Year". Theresa's teacher had all the members of her class write nominations as part of a learning exercise. A certain number of compositions were subsequently submitted to the selection committee.

Theresa's mom won! Carol was named "Mother of the Year" for 1978 at Edwards Air Force Base. General Conley, the commander, presented the award to Mom at a breakfast. The best, though, was the feeling and thoughts that little Theresa described and wrote in her composition transcribed here.

WHY I THINK MY MOTHER SHOULD BE MOTHER OF THE YEAR

I think my mother should be mother of the year because she makes good food for our family and makes all kinds of clothes for our family, takes us to model airplane contests. And takes all the racket in the house. She has to pack most of the house when we are going to move when our dad is gone. She takes us to church, ball and scout functions. Takes care of our St. Bernard when we are at school. But most of all she's our mom. She's a mom of 11 kids.

By Theresa Kerzie
Grade 5
April 20, 1978

WHEN I WAS LITTLE

Input from Matt

These stories I'm writing about aren't really related in any way. Just some vivid memories I had when I was little.

The first one brings me back to 1975 when we were living on Edwards A.F.B., at the house on Lindbergh Drive. Dad, always the first one awake, was usually out the door before anyone else got up. Let me tell you, it wasn't any different on weekends, either. In order to get the family going on weekend chores, my Dad's favorite way to get us moving was to play "reveille" through his cupped hands. Yes, he would stop by each bedroom door, on the way to the kitchen, stopping only long enough to play what most military personnel hear at boot camp. I know this sounds like a cruel way of coming out of a deep sleep but it sure got the heart pumping. Besides, I'm sure, Dad had a lot of fun doing it. My fellow work colleague Joe says that Dad got this from the movie The Great Santini (rent it sometime and get flashbacks).

You might ask what reminded me of this moment. Well, I'm usually the first one awake at our house; you take a guess what happens!

The second? I remember one particular trip we took to Seattle, in the mid 1970s. We were at Grandma Kerzie's house. It was a slow day and the kids were looking for something to do, so we went to the back yard to play. We noticed that Grandma's garage door was open, so we decided to go in. We found ourselves in Grandpa's workshop. Some of us were admiring some of Grandpa's old dusty tools. He had a lot of them. I wasn't interested in his tools. But what I really remember, at that time, was the old musty smell of Grandpa's old workshop.

Next time you're in Palmdale, go into Dad's garage, close your eyes, and take a whiff. It'll bring back memories.

SIBLING CARE, LOVE, AND PRIDE

Input from Todd

DAD'S NOTES

All the kids have been close, even the older ones with the youngest. Like all children, there were differences as they were growing up, but comparatively few. To this day, the family remains as one even though many miles separate many of the members.

Our oldest son, Mike, was ten years old when Dad shipped out for Vietnam, a year-long assignment away from the family. The family then was made up of seven boys plus little Theresa, the only girl at the time. Todd was the youngest, at fourteen months. Little Mike assumed the role of Dad and displayed a maturity that very much belied his young age. Mike and baby Todd established a special bond that year which became obvious as the years went on.

Turn the calendar from the days of little Mike and baby Todd to about thirty-one years later...

Mike was on duty at the Pentagon during the terrorist strike September 11, 2001. His duty station was located very close to the impact point and as a result he became a very busy man for the next few hours. All Mom and Dad could do was to watch the events as they unfolded on TV with horror, and hope for the best as communications, of course, were down in Mike's immediate area. Talk about a gut wrench for all that time as the calls started coming in from near and far, sobbing kids concerned about their oldest brother. It was almost four hours after the impact that Mike was able to call out that he was ok.

Todd's e-mail to Mike, a month after the event, is transcribed here and summarizes the title of this story.

> *Mike,*
>
> *You have always been my lifelong "Buddy" and a TRUE HERO of mine. I seem to have been following you around all my life. Maybe that's why I'm in the service, like you. I can remember going and watching you run cross-country on D-Hill, going to wrestling matches, baseball games, etc. I can distinctly remember you holding my head in your blood-soaked T-shirt after I got hit in the head with a rock. I can remember you helping me build my first model airplanes and helping me launch them with my hand in a cast. I can remember you taking me to your ROTC drills down in Alameda in the MG. But most of all while growing up, I can remember you being a true leader of our family, taking care of all of your siblings by putting our concerns before yours.*
>
> *I have to echo Dad and congratulate you on your actions resulting in the awarding of the "Soldier's Medal". When we heard of the tragedies on September 11th, and did not hear from you, my thoughts were, "Mike is in the middle of it, pulling another selfless deed and helping someone else out!" I know you are proud to be a soldier. I just hope the Americans realize the selfless acts the servicemen and women do on a daily basis to protect their freedoms. I would be remiss if I did not thank you for the leadership and example you were growing up!*
>
> *Thanks, Buddy! And Semper Fi!*
> *Todd*

SIBLINGS, PEER PRESSURE, AND MORE PRIDE

Mom and Dad worked hard on the older boys, in an attempt to install the values of good education and learning. Mike had just finished his first year of college and Mark was about to enter the halls of higher learning when the family made its final geographical move. It was decided then that Cal Poly University Pomona was a good choice for a university as the school had a widely varied curriculum and was relatively inexpensive. Cal Poly was not Ivy League but some research proved that the school had a very good reputation. All the children followed Mike and Mark and all eventually graduated (more or less) by the numbers. Was this a form of peer pressure? We think so.

The campus was close enough for weekend commutes, but let Mike finish a more than thirteen-year-long history of sibling peer pressure and pride in his letter, reproduced below. His letter, with the introduction, was published in the Fall '96 issue of the Cal Poly University school newspaper, *POLYTRENDS*.

AKIN ALUMNI

THE ELEVENTH SIBLING GRADUATES FROM CAL POLY POMONA

The Kerzies could probably start their own alumni chapter; Michelle Kerzie was the last of 11 siblings to graduate from Cal Poly Pomona in Spring Quarter. In honor of the occasion, her brother Michael ('83) donated $2,125 to the Alumni Brick Wall of Fame Scholarship Endowment Fund and requested a special section on the Walk of Fame set aside for the Kerzie graduates.

The Alumni Association challenges you to follow Michael Kerzie's lead:

On June 9, 1996, my youngest sister will graduate. Michelle will receive recognition not only for an individual achievement, but also for a family achievement. You see, she will be the last of the eleven children of David and Carol Kerzie to graduate from Cal Poly Pomona. My sister and I have a special relationship. We have both graduated from the same college, spanning thirteen years. All of us have paid our own way, some through military scholarships, others through hard work during the summer and school year. Michelle was fortunate to receive a basketball scholarship after her first year. She continued to work as a veterinarian assistant and lifeguard to help pay her way.

Our father and mother instilled strong values in us: education, hard work, hard play, and most of all, to never give up. There was no pressure for Michelle to graduate; she was supported by our parents and the rest of us. On many occasions, my parents would drive hundreds of miles to attend Michelle's basketball games. Eventually, she was picked NCAA All-Conference Second

Team. All of us have been successful in our own special way; some fly, some are engineers, some are dentists, some manage restaurants, some are in the military, and some are teachers. Each has been successful, and an education from Cal Poly Pomona helped. We all wish Michelle the best of luck.

I would like to give the Alumni Brick Walk of Fame Scholarship Endowment Fund $2,125 to support student scholarships. This is a small price to pay for what the school has provided our family. In return, I request that our bricks be laid in a special place in order from left to right, from oldest to youngest:

Michael J. Kerzie '83, Aerospace Engineering
Mark G. Kerzie '84, Computer Science
Matthew J. Kerzie '85, Art
Martin L. Kerzie '86, Biology
Thomas M. Kerzie '89, Political Science
Timothy J. Kerzie '93, Hotel & Restaurant Management
Theresa M. Kerzie '91, Liberal Studies
Todd A. Kerzie '91, Physical Education
Theodore D. Kerzie '92 Aerospace Engineering
Mary E. Kerzie '94, Liberal Studies
Michelle A. Kerzie '96, Liberal Studies

Thank You,
Michael J. Kerzie

LOOKING BACK

Input from Mike

From Michael Kerzie, HQ US Army, Tue. 19 Mar 2002 07:46:36

Happy Birthday Dad,

BIRTHDAYS

Birthdays are special for lots of reasons: A reminder of the day we were born, to thank God for keeping us safe for another year, and an opportunity to remember those who have gone before us. Every birthday is special around the Kerzie family. As the family gets stretched, it has become obvious the things you really miss. Mom's angel food cake with strawberries and pink ice cream for starters. Although the presents were always great, it was getting together to sing a birthday song what really meant most. In the old days, it seemed that every month, we were having a birthday to celebrate. If we include the grandkids, it's now about every other week. Mom can tell you when they all are and does a great job in getting cards/gifts out in time.

Truly our family has been blessed and healthy, considering all the accidents we have had including: tricycles, bicycles, motorcycles, cars, trucks, campers, hang gliders, sailplanes, helicopters, and airplanes. Why we never crashed Mom's station wagon going 100 mph on South Base, we will never know, but we did eventually crash it into a mulberry tree. Yes we have all been lucky. Mike was born on Grandma Kerzie's birthday, Cindi was born on Dad's birthday, Mark was born on Bob Barker's birthday, and so on...

Not sure how many other grandkids will be born into this family, but one thing is for sure, there is a lot of history in this one.

Love, Mike

Dave's note: Mark, our second oldest, had just graduated from the university and was a newlywed when his story (as he writes it), took place.

"DON'T BURN THE HOUSE DOWN"

Input from Mark

It was the spring of 1984. Sherri and I had been married only a few months when Mom and Dad challenged us with one of our first big responsibilities outside of our new home. By this time, Dad had been retired from the service for about five years and had established his roots with an aerospace company in Palmdale, California. His company offered Dad an opportunity to attend a symposium in Europe - an opportunity he really couldn't refuse! Could Mom go along? You bet - work combined with a short vacation away from home - a second honeymoon yet! While we were growing up, our parents rarely took trips alone. Part of the problem included what do with all the kids while they were gone. Sherri and I took on that challenge.

There wasn't too much time to plan and prepare, but that didn't matter. It was decided that the best approach would be to keep the kids where they were. So, Sherri and I packed a week's worth of clothes and headed for the big house. Everything still looked the same; I even got my old bedroom back (sleeping bag on the living room floor). Mom had the house ticking like clockwork so the turnover was quite simple. We spent some time getting briefed on emergency procedures, points of contact, and going over the schedules of all the kids that were still at home. Then, we sent our parents on their merry way.

The week was filled with all kinds of events. It was the end of the school year, and we discovered that those times could be quite busy. Needless to say, all went off without a hitch; this was way too easy. Towards the end of the week, we discussed our traditional Sunday evening dinner. The college kids were coming home for the weekend and Sherri was up for making the event happen, so there was no reason to break tradition. We assured all standard invitees that the event was still a go and started the normal preparations.

That Sunday included one of those beautiful Palmdale spring afternoons. Pleasant temperatures, no wind, birds circling in thermals overhead, pretty desert landscape – just one of those days that you were glad you lived in Palmdale. By late afternoon, Father Steve had completed his Sunday duties and was headed over to the house. The older kids, after finishing up their jobs for the day, started to arrive with their girlfriends. Eventually, we had a quorum and could start the festivities.

One of our family favorites was rolled flank steak and that was appropriately placed on the menu as the main entrée. All this, naturally, dictated the requirement for our outdoor BBQ. Those were the days when the standard operation included using charcoal. Tom, who has always had a passion for fire, volunteered to get the BBQ going. Tom always did a good job of setting up a hot bed of coals, but this weekend he seemed to be having some problems. The coals would not light. Tom and Father Steve were observed discussing the matter. It appeared that Tom was offering up a solution and Father Steve was agreeing with an obvious nod of approval. Very soon thereafter, Tom and Father Steve came walking out of the garage with a metal can of gasoline. Tom ever- so-gently poured some of the gas on the dead set of coals.

The coals weren't quite dead. The fire immediately jumped up to the source and to keep from getting burned Tom dropped the can of gas on the porch. Within seconds, the fire had engulfed the can of gas and the flames were getting precariously close to the patio overhang. Father Steve's first instinct was to get the fire away from the house, so he kicked the can into the middle of the backyard. Discovering that the ball of fire was now burning a hole in Dad's grass, it was kicked again into the natural area of the backyard - right into the middle of some large sagebrush. I didn't realize until then how fast sagebrush would burn and it looked as though the blaze might spread.

The commotion attracted the rest of the family who then immediately started brainstorming on how to put the fire out. The first idea was the garden hose; it was hooked up and the water turned on. Fireman Father Steve ran to the fire with the hose only to discover it was about three feet too short to reach the fire. Immediately, others came out of the house with bowls and cups to fill with water. That didn't work and the fire was getting bigger. Then Matt remembered the ten-gallon lemonade juice jug Mom always kept at the sink for our regular drinking needs. That did the trick.

Everyone's nerves started to calm and we eventually extinguished the whole fire. Unfortunately, all the sagebrush took a fairly significant hit. But that was the least of our worries. What would Dad think about our little accident? The next two hours were spent digging out roots and filling in the hole; it was a good team effort. If one didn't know any better, there was never a bush fire to begin with. We had our traditional Sunday evening dinner, Father Steve went back to his church, Mom and Dad came home happy from their trip, and Sherri and I headed back to our own place. We didn't drop the entire adventure on our parents all at once, but eventually the story came out. Often, the extra little pieces of the story came out during discussions of prior family close calls and how Father Steve somehow seemed to always be involved.

ONE OF ELEVEN

INPUT FROM MARY

Our lives all started at an obscure bus stop,
And then soon came the Kerzie Family crop!

8 boys and 3 girls is the last and final score,
Mom and Dad surely won, we need not say anymore!

Growing up one of eleven, not too many get to see,
All the fun and enjoyment of a large family!

Some looked at our folks and just thought they were crazy,
But they certainly made sure not one of us was lazy!

We all had our roles and daily chores to get done,
And when they were done we had quite a bit of fun!

From dishes to yard work, and the many loads of clothes,
How they kept it all fair, of course, nobody knows!

The emergency rooms seemed to know us all by name,
As broken bones and stitches were a part of Kerzie fame!

Our school years went by, even sometimes hard to recall,
Each one of us has made it through the Cal Poly hall!

Most of us played sports or were on a cheering squad,
Mom or Dad and often both were always there to cheer us on!

Many of the great memories have come here and gone,
From camping trips to models, the list could go on!

We have all chosen our careers and moved out on our own,
Many have had kids themselves, our family sure has grown!

We owe it to Mom and Dad, the best parents of them all,
They showed us how to love, be proud, and to always stand tall!

NUMBER ELEVEN

Input from Michelle

My parents were blessed on August 4, 1973 with their eleventh child. That was me: Michelle Ann Kerzie. You cannot begin to imagine the memories I have from growing up in a family of eleven children, and, better yet, being the youngest of eleven. When people ask me how many brothers and sisters I have, my answer is always 'ten'. I have eight brothers and two sisters. After I tell them this, I wait for their response. Often, I hear an "OH, MY GOSH!" or "Where do you fall in the line?" When I tell them that I am the youngest, the baby, their first response is often, "You must have been spoiled!" My older brothers and sisters may agree with that, but let me argue my point that being the youngest wasn't always easy. It did, however help me to be a smarter individual who makes better decisions in life.

There wasn't a time that I remember my parents saying, "Why don't you try to be like your sister and...," They encouraged us to be individuals. Our parents didn't pressure us to be doctors, lawyers or scientists. All they asked was for me to go to college, receive a degree, and become a good citizen and a contributor to society. Actually, being the youngest of eleven has made me the person I am today. I wouldn't trade those ten sets of footsteps I had to follow for anything. We were very fortunate to have parents that loved us, cared for us, and taught us values that carry us into our adult life. We didn't have the material things growing up, but we certainly had each other. If it ever seemed as though I had no friends, I always knew I had ten of them at home. And now, if you ever want to come back to Mom and Dad Kerzie's house, let them know when you're going to come, when you're going to leave, and how many are going to be home for dinner. You know Mom and Dad will always welcome you with floor space, and Mom will always have dinner waiting.

AN OPEN LETTER TO MY CHILDREN

Dear kids,

As your mother and I enter the autumn (or maybe even the winter) of our lives, it is probably appropriate to write a few words describing some of our feelings.

First: I guess I'm kind of sad that your Mom and I couldn't supply you all with a lot of material things as you were growing up but we really didn't have the means to do that. We sense that some of you are maybe trying to rectify that with respect to your own children, and that's ok, just don't spoil them. Let the kids appreciate what they have. Recall the many dinners we had where one marshmallow for dessert was a treat, and I don't believe you all suffered as a consequence.

Second: Your Mother and I have tried to instill in you all the value of education. Most of you understand this and we are so proud of the way you all have assumed the tasks of higher learning. Remember; learning is a never-ending process, keep pressing. It is fun. Hopefully, you will continue to instill these precepts in your own children.

Third: It has become apparent, as your Mom and Dad stand back and observe you kids and your own families, that we may have been too demanding in your upbringing with respect to organization, discipline, structure, and orientation with success. Are we thinking this because we are older? Maybe. But you need to back off once in a while to view the sky, clouds, and stars, and reflect.

Fourth: Always be a good person and be good to others; just a kind word to others goes a long way. You all know the difference between right and wrong, and we had many discussions while you were growing up about integrity. Practice your faith. If you tend to stray, get back to it. Set a good example for your children.

Fifth: Words can't describe the love your Mother and I have had for all you kids. We are so proud of all of you, not only for your individual achievements, but for the way you have all matured as positive and caring examples in society. What a joy you all have been. Each and everyone remain special in our hearts.

Sixth: I can't close without writing about your mother. She is the best thing that ever happened to me. As I tried to describe earlier, I fell "head over heels" for her the first time I saw her, and I love her more as each day passes. I am so lucky to have her, and you kids are so fortunate to have her for a mom.

Anyhow kids, I know that I'm preaching to the choir, just trying to reinforce some of the things we talked about and learned together as we were all growing up.

Keep on doing good works.

All my love,
Dad

Printed in the United States
53011LVS00004B/478-495